The Collection 2016

An Hachette UK Company
www.hachette.co.uk

First published in Great Britain in 2015 by Hamlyn,
a division of Octopus Publishing Group Ltd, Carmelite House
50 Victoria Embankment, London EC4Y 0DZ

www.octopusbooks.co.uk

Cartoons

British Cartoon Archive

Cartoons supplied by British Cartoon Archive
Cartoons compiled by John Field

This edition produced for
The Book People Ltd
Catteshall Manor, Catteshall Lane
Godalming, Surrey, GU7 1UU

ISBN 978 0 600 63286 3

A CIP catalogue record for this book is available from the British Library.
Printed and bound in China
1 3 5 7 9 10 8 6 4 2

The Collection 2016

compiled by John Field
foreword by Judith Miller

EXPRESS NEWSPAPERS

hamlyn

Contents

Foreword

Judith Miller
Antiques Expert

For me, opening an edition of *Giles: The Collection* reminds me of growing up in a wool town in the Scottish Borders in the 1950s. I was born into a small tenement flat in the centre of Galashiels and the characters take me back to those permanently sunny days (who am I kidding?), playing in the communal back yard with a "raggle-taggle" assortment of children and adults. There was even the pub on the corner, The Auld Mill, that was men-only – even Grandma would have thought twice about crossing that threshold.

My father loved Giles and I remember him sitting in front of the fire chuckling at the gentle slaying of politicians or the "stuck-up" English – the city chaps with bowler hats – while I was too young to understand.

These days humour can be cruel, oblique and elitist, but Giles's cartoons covered family life, politics and popular culture with a gentler twist – while still making a salient point. It is social commentary of the top drawer.

Giles obviously had a deep love of Britain and perfectly captured the nuances of British life, from the economic booms and busts, strikes, scandals, drunks, the hoi-poloi and the toffs to that most stressful of times – the family holiday. His fictional family displayed all the ups and downs of family life. But he also covered the royal family, presidents and politicians.

With Giles it is often not the central image but some incident on the sidelines that captures your attention – like the child putting toothpaste into Grandma's tea or the expressions on the animals' faces as they observe some scene. And didn't we all have an Auntie Vera?

Of course the all-time favourite is Grandma and there were quite a few Grandmas when I was growing up – always in black, with hat and coat on, brolly at the ready, fox fur round the throat and arms folded. And the face when someone passed by who lived "up on the hill" and was "no better than she ought to be" was perfectly captured by Giles.

As we look back it is amazing how much has changed in society and yet how much has stayed the same. I'm sure that our enduring fascination for and love of Giles is nostalgia. He captured the Britain we have loved and in some cases lost.

As an inveterate collector, I look at Giles's cartoons and they bring back all the memories of different times in my life. And as a collector I would recommend searching out some Giles originals – they are a record of the late 20th century and are still very affordable. Buy now – you heard it here.

Judith Nuttie

Giles's Institutions – Introduction

There is little doubt that every country has its own institutions, traditions and characteristics, that give its people a strong sense of national identity. This year's Giles annual concentrates on some of his cartoons which relate to a number of institutions considered fundamental to how we British see ourselves as a separate people.

With this in mind, the theme chosen for this year's annual uses Giles's cartoons as a means of exploring and illustrating six institutions generally recognized as being an important part of national life throughout the United Kingdom: the Monarchy, the BBC, the Pub, the Church, Football and Bobbies on the Beat.

Finally, in looking at Giles's pictorial record of our country's life, we must remember that much time has passed since it was created and we now live in a more multicultural and diverse society. The national landscape portrayed by Giles has, therefore, changed to some degree, but most people will feel that the institutions shown in this collection of his work still play an important and defining role in today's wider society within Britain.

The Monarchy

In his work, Giles produced a number of cartoons portraying members of the royal family and sometimes marked such things as the birth of a new member with a specific cartoon. He obviously enjoyed Prince Philip's penchant for occasionally being a bit outspoken and once portrayed the Queen taking part in a demonstration, as a racehorse owner, threatening to go on strike against a new betting tax.

However, their inclusion in a Giles cartoon seems to have been accepted quite happily by the royal family.

Giles's *Express* colleague, Peter Tory, reported in his various books that a member of the royal family would frequently ask for a copy of a cartoon in which they appeared, resulting in over 30 being in royal ownership.

The BBC

Giles's cartoons often included references to popular BBC programmes at the time, including *Till Death Us Do Part*, *The Good Life* and *Match of the Day*, as well as to different personalities such as Robin Day and Selina Scott, who caused a sensation at the time as a presenter on the first broadcasting breakfast television. One special character, Alf Garnett, the star of *Till Death Us Do Part*, appeared in his own right in at least two cartoons.

Presumably through his cartoon work, Giles became good friends with many people in the entertainment world and there are photographs of him in his home at Hillbrow Farm, in Suffolk, with some of them, including Tommy Cooper, Eric Sykes and Johnny Speight – the scriptwriter of *Till Death Us Do Part*.

The Pub

Giles was a great fan of British pubs and loved to portray them, with their great mix of British life, as the setting for his humour. He often frequented his nearest local, Witnesham's Barley Mow, about half a mile from his farm, but he could also be regularly found at nearby Tuddenham's Fountain, where he was a member of the darts team. He also visited a number of pubs in Ipswich, where he had his studio, and in the surrounding countryside, and is known to have visited a range of hostelries when in London. It was not surprising or unusual, therefore, for a pub cartoon to be based upon one of his many haunts.

There is little doubt that Giles, today, would have been greatly saddened to know that the future of this British institution, despite being an iconic feature of our country, is under threat – it was reported last summer that British pubs are closing down at a rate of 31 a week. However, many are accepting the changes and becoming more family friendly and pub cuisine is now, usually, something to be applauded. I am sure that these changes would have given Giles much material for his work and it is a great pity he is not here to chronicle them.

The Church
The beauty and intricacies of ecclesiastical architecture gave Giles much opportunity to use his drawing skills and the various characters involved with church life, from the bishops, vicars and church wardens to the broad range of parishioners, provided considerable material for his work.

Although his studio was in the middle of Ipswich, he lived a few miles outside the town and was, no doubt, very aware of the importance of the church in village life. This comes out strongly in his 'country church' cartoons.

I am not aware of any great evidence that Giles went to church on a regular basis, but he is buried in the quiet village churchyard at Tuddenham, a few miles from his home, with a very simple headstone just saying 'Carl Giles OBE Born 29th Sept 1916 Died 27th Aug 1995', in addition to details about his wife, Joan.

Football
Although football has now become a worldwide sport, there is no doubt that the game has been ingrained in the British DNA for longer than any other country. Although Giles sometimes showed his strong disapproval of football hooliganism in his cartoons, he was a great supporter of the sport and, of course, was delighted when his home team Ipswich won the FA Cup in 1978. He marked this win with Grandma, an ardent local supporter, ready to go up to Wembley on the Saturday morning of the match and the following day showed her returning home with Butch the dog carrying the Cup in his mouth.

Bobbies on the Beat
The final institution covered in this annual is the British 'Bobby'. Along with the vicar, the bobby (usually with his distinctive helmet) is a mainstay of life in 'Giles's country'. Giles was well-known (in the nicest sense) to the local police force and in many of his police cartoons it was not unusual for a particular officer to be recognizable as an actual bobby on the beat. Sometimes when this happened Giles would send a copy of the cartoon to the bobby involved. In addition to his newspaper cartoons, he was asked on many occasions to produce cartoons for various local police activities such as police and CID dinner dances. This he did free of charge, as he did for the many cartoons and drawings he produced for a wide range of charities and other worthy bodies.

In conclusion, I hope that this year's collection not only succeeds in illustrating Giles's sense of humour and ability to capture in his drawings a wide range of people and incidents in our national life, but also shows his obvious affection for the traditions and deep-rooted institutions of our country.

John Field

The Monarchy

In the year following her succession to the throne, Queen Elizabeth II and Prince Philip undertook a six-month grand tour of the Commonwealth. This cartoon welcomed them back.

WELCOME HOME

Sunday Express, May 16, 1954

In 1957, Elizabeth II made a state visit to the USA for the first time since becoming queen. The focus of her visit was the first permanent English settlement in America – Jamestown, Virginia, which was celebrating its 350th anniversary. The Queen and Prince Philip also visited Washington DC, where they met President Eisenhower, and New York City, where she spoke at the UN.

"Elmer! I don't give a damn how pro-Monarchist you are—take it off and take it back where you rented it at once."

Daily Express, October 20, 1957

12 At the Chelsea Flower Show, three days before this cartoon appeared, Prince Philip had roared with laughter when two press photographers got soaked as a lawn sprinkler suddenly started to work. It was reported that no one admitted to having seen him actually press the button which controlled the sprayer but it was noted that the Prince "was the nearest".

"Psst! Keep that —thing out of his reach until we've got our pictures."

Daily Express, May 28, 1959

"With the greatest respect for your tattered nerves – PUT IT OUT!"

Daily Express, February 16, 1960

14 Wedding preparations for the marriage of Princess Margaret and Antony Armstrong-Jones, which took place two days later, caused major traffic congestion in central London with people wishing to see the decorations. Thousands of cars were expected to try to enter the city centre for the occasion itself and some 7,000 police officers were brought in to control the crowds.
Maybe Prince Philip felt that having such a driver would have helped him get through to the service at Westminster Abbey on time.

"Fortunately, His Royal Highness's new ex-trick-cyclist chauffeur will not be driving at the wedding."

Daily Express, May 4, 1960

Prince Philip, a keen sailor, served as President of the Royal Yachting Association and also as President of the Commonwealth Games Federation during this period. As shown on the cartoon dated 28th May, of the previous year (see page 12), the Prince was not too concerned if a press photographer occasionally got a bit wet in the course of duty.

"Good picture, Harry – just as you were saying 'He's bluffing, he wouldn't dare!'"

Daily Express, August 4, 1960

Viscount Linley, the first child of Princess Margaret and Antony Armstrong-Jones, was born two days earlier.

"Whoops! Jock's trod on something sharp."

Sunday Express, November 5, 1961

Lord Beaverbrook, then proprietor of the Express Newspapers, was criticised by Prince Philip for his newspaper's coverage of the royal family. Giles produced this cartoon despite the fact that the Lord was Giles's boss, or perhaps because of it?

"The Express is a bloody awful newspaper," said the Duke. "Ah, well," said Lord B., as they trotted him off to the Tower, "at least he takes it or he wouldn't know it was a bloody awful newspaper."

Daily Express, March 22, 1962

This shows a group of young people on their way to the Isle of Wight Festival. The day before this cartoon appeared, it was reported that Prince Philip had given a lift to two newlyweds on their honeymoon.

"That's great, Ma'am. Thanks for the lift."

Daily Express, August 27, 1970

The day before the government had discussed rent rebate schemes (see page 23).

19

"I hardly feel, dear, that because the sink at Balmoral hasn't been working properly since your great-great-grandmother's time, it justifies claiming a rent rebate."

Daily Express, November 5, 1970

This demonstration, in which Giles has included the Queen, refers to racehorse owners' unhappiness at a proposed betting tax on bookies. Note the rival demonstration in the distance which relates to an avant-garde musical at the time that received considerable public comment for its sex-related topics and scenes of nudity.

"The show must go on..."

Daily Express, November 19, 1970

The weekend before, the Queen and Queen Mother had been travelling back to Windsor Castle from a private dinner party when they were stopped by a motorcycle policeman uncertain about the flashing blue light on the roof of their car. The use of these lights is not normal procedure for private occasions, causing the policeman's confusion.

"Why do I have reason to suspect it is not the Queen? Because the Queen would not use an expression like 'Shove off'."

Sunday Express, February 21, 1971

Prince Philip's 50th birthday. The reference to Tiny relates to Roland "Tiny" Rowland, a British businessman at the time with a reputation for hard bargaining, who had become generally unpopular in many quarters.

"Philip! It isn't Tiny's fault everybody is printing books about your first half hundred."

Daily Express, June 10, 1971

The previous day, the government had considered a White Paper proposing a national rent rebate scheme which, for the first time, had the potential to provided rebates for private tenants. Presumably this had caused Prince Philip to change his view expressed in the cartoon eight months earlier (see page 19).

"Philip, did you telephone the council about this new rent assistance bill?"

Daily Express, July 15, 1971

"At the first sound of a Royal Flush we strike up with 'All Through The Night' Prestissimo!"

Daily Express, July 13, 1972

An unusual view of the front facade of Buckingham Palace. When he was 14, Prince Andrew went on a school exchange holiday to Toulouse, France. He stated that, as part of an elaborate ploy to keep his identity secret, his father was a gentleman farmer, his mother did not work and that his name was Edward. The family he stayed with was in on the secret.

"We must teach Your Royal Highness that it is imprudent to fill in forms: 'My mum doesn't work'."

Daily Express, October 3, 1974

"They've a pretty strong picket line – the Queen, the Queen Mother, Lord Derby, Peter O'Sullevan, to name but a few."

Daily Express, November 7, 1974

The Queen and Prince Philip had just returned from an historic six-day visit to Japan, being the first visit by a reigning British monarch. Presumably the Prince had taken a keen interest in Japanese martial arts whilst there.

"On your feet, corporal – I'm sure His Royal Highness only gave you a karate chop for fun."

Daily Express, May 13, 1975

28   The Queen and Prince Philip were on an official visit to Antigua. The previous week, the Prince had been criticised by some MPs. about the "doom-laden" views he had expressed in a broadcast about the future of Britain.

"HRH is in one of his doom-watch moods this morning – hear that rude little word from below when you muffed that?"

Daily Express, October 30, 1977

Farrah Fawcett-Majors was a beautiful American actress, who starred in the popular television programme *Charlie's Angels* and was aged 31 at the time. Margaret Trudeau, aged 30, was the former wife of Pierre Trudeau, Prime Minister of Canada, who was 30 years older. Seduced by her youth and beauty, the Canadians fell in love with her, just as they had been charmed by her charismatic husband. She had separated from Pierre a few months before this cartoon appeared. William "Willie" Hamilton, then aged 61, was a British Labour politician who was known for his strong republican views. No doubt the 30-year-old Prince Charles, still unmarried at the time, felt that this would make for an interesting weekend.

"Fawcett-Majors Farrah – Trudeau Margaret – Hamilton Willie. Please come here a moment, Charles."

Earlier that week, a painting titled *Near Stoke-by-Nayland*, until then thought to be by the landscape artist John Constable, was attributed to his son, Lionel.

"Now you've taken up art, Charles, please pay special attention to the signature and avoid the same confusion as Constable and his son."

Sunday Express, October 8, 1978

Following intrusive action by the tabloid press, who constantly followed Diana Spencer's movements, Prince Charles told reporters staked out nearby: "A thoroughly nasty new year to your editors". Within two months the engagement of Prince Charles and Diana was officially announced.

"I've passed your message to the Editor, Sir – and one from me for sending me on this story."

Daily Express, January 6, 1981

A few days after the Queen and Prince Philip returned from a visit to America, Charles and Diana travelled to Australia and New Zealand for a six-week official visit. The Princess insisted on taking their nine-month old baby, Prince William, with them. This cartoon illustrates Giles's obvious pleasure at drawing an interesting range of military and ceremonial uniforms.

Daily Express, March 12, 1983

"You'll get YOUR ticket when your father learns what you've sprayed on my sergeant's back, Your Royal Highness."

Daily Express, February 25, 1988

This was the Queen Mother's 88th birthday – maybe Grandma was of a similar age.

"Can her Majesty slip out for a quick half of bitter for her birthday?"

Daily Express, August 4, 1988

The BBC

"And I say unto you, even at this very moment there is one among us whose thoughts turn not from the paths of greed and wickedness."

Sunday Express, October 2, 1955

There was some debate at this time about the showing of violence on television. Fyfe Robertson and Alan Whicker were two very popular reporters on BBC television. Robertson had an easy-going manner when reporting while Whicker was known for his subtle brand of satire and social commentary.

TV's fearless Fyfe Robertson and Two-gun Whicker inviting crime-soaked members of the public to give their views on the B.B.C.'s decision to abolish violence from its programmes

Daily Express, March 31, 1960

The BBC had arranged with the Moscow TV Central Network for the Trooping of the Colour to be broadcast live to the Russians the day before. Earlier in the year, the BBC had broadcast Moscow's May Day Parade to the UK.

"Technically speaking, Farquharson, to the TV viewers in Moscow we're just another 'Western'."

Sunday Express, June 11, 1961

Z Cars was a BBC drama series centred on the work of a mobile uniformed police force in the Merseyside area. It had started in January of the previous year and ran for 16 years. The series differed from earlier police dramas by injecting a new element of harsh realism into the image of the police, which some found unwelcome.

"Since you started shouting at them like they do in Z cars the tea's been simply 'orrible."

Daily Express, September 5, 1963

"That's all we want on top of his price war – the B.B.C. to go and cancel his blessed Z cars"

Daily Express, April 1, 1965

40 The "Early Bird", the first commercial communications satellite, was placed in orbit one month earlier. The day before this cartoon appeared, the newspapers reported that the police had used the satellite in their search for three great train robbers still at large.

"Can we bounce an announcement off Early Bird satellite that the lady here has lost a pair of light mauve gloves?"

Daily Express, May 4, 1965

This refers to the very popular television programme *Till Death Us Do Part* in which the main character, Alf Garnett, used this term of endearment when referring to his wife. Obviously this gentleman made the big mistake of using it towards his own wife.

"Sending me to bed before that programme starts won't stop me calling you a silly old moo."

Daily Express, January 10, 1967

42 The BBC drama *The Forsyte Saga* was an extremely popular programme, which ran for 26 episodes. It was so popular that some clergy altered the time of their Sunday sermon to fit around it. The two saboteurs were important characters on the rival ITV channel. Sooty was a small yellow bear puppet whose programme on the BBC was cancelled the previous year and he moved to ITV where the programme was aired until 1992. Ena Sharples was a central character in the extremely successful ITV programme *Coronation Street* which, of course, is still running.

"B.B.C. Security? Reporting sabotage by ITV – we've got Sooty and Ena Sharples cropping up in the Forsyte Saga"

Daily Express, September 13, 1968

The following day President Richard Nixon started a two-day informal visit to London, met Prime Minister Harold Wilson and was received by the Queen at Buckingham Palace.

"Now I've seen everything. Powdering their little red noses for colour TV."

Sunday Express, February 23, 1969

This was a period that saw industrial militancy at the BBC, with staff threatening to take strike action.

"Aren't you on strike yet, boy?"

The infamous character in BBC's *Till Death Us Do Part,* Alf Garnett, played by actor Warren Mitchell, and his "family" appeared in this year's Royal Variety Performance at the London Palladium in a sketch written by Johnny Speight.

"Anyone who has had as much to do with horses as yer actual Queen Mother will understand most of the words in your script, Mr. Garnett."

Daily Express, October 5, 1972

Lord Hill was the chairman of the BBC Governors at this time and Mary Whitehouse was an activist who expressed strong opposition to increased sexual liberalism in mainstream British broadcasting, which she considered encouraged a too permissive society.

"I, Lord Hill, do promise Mary, never to allow the pornographic Old Testament to be heard on BBC religious programmes."

Daily Express, October 8, 1972

A judge, dealing with an action in a professional football match which resulted with a player being sent off and having to pay a fine, declared, after watching a replay of the film on television three times in court, that it was clear that the referee had made a mistake.

"BBC? I'd like an action replay when my husband comes home – I've just seen him in the second row Block B working late at the office."

Sunday Express, October 22, 1972

48 It was reported the day before that all BBC producers and staff were issued with a pamphlet giving them guidance on the use of swearing and bad language in programmes. Probably Mary Whitehouse had been active again.

"Actually Charlie has read the notice, but that lamp he picked up was a trifle warm."

Daily Express, February 8, 1973

A new four-year deal in 1979 split the football match rights between the BBC and ITV and as a consequence *Match of the Day* was moved to Sunday afternoons for the 1980–1 and 1982–3 seasons.

"One thing about moving 'Match of the Day' to Sunday – it gets 'em home earlier for lunch"

Sunday Express, September 7, 1980

It had just been announced that the BBC was to commence breakfast TV in a few weeks' time and on the day this cartoon appeared independent Channel 4 television was launched as a public service broadcaster, funded entirely from commercial revenue.

"Let me get this right – you want to come in an hour later because of Breakfast TV and knock off an hour earlier to see Channel 4?"

Daily Express, November 2, 1982

The Good Life was a BBC television programme based upon a young couple who decide to leave behind the rat race and become self-sufficient by converting their garden into a small farm and growing their own crops – with varying degrees of success.

"Remember last night? 1983 is going to be different – we're all going to live like they do in The Good Life on TV."

Daily Express, January 4, 1983

The BBC's "Breakfast Time" started the day before with Selina Scott as a major presenter and Debbie Rix as a newsreader.

"You'll have to start getting to bed earlier to get down in time to see your Debbie and Selina."

Early morning in the Giles family household on the day that ITV commenced its breakfast television programme, *TV-am*, just two weeks after the BBC had started its breakfast programme.

"Dad, I've just counted up – we've got six more people than we've got in the family."

Daily Express, February 1, 1983

The first broadcasting of Parliament commenced experimentally the next day and was made permanent soon after. Of course there was a strict ban on all advertising, hence the cleaner's concern about her labelled box of washing powder.

"It's not Black Rod, M'Lord – the lady has left her box of Persil just behind the throne."

Daily Express, January 22, 1985

Frank Bough became a first presenter of the BBC's breakfast programme, along with Selina Scott, and was chosen for his very smooth, relaxed and professional approach to live broadcasting. The ITV morning broadcast had a rather more light-hearted approach compared with the BBC version and Giles is probably making this point with this cartoon.

"That wasn't funny, Selina – we allocate those sort of jokes to the other channel."

Daily Express, November 7, 1985

Mary Whitehouse was an activist who expressed strong criticism about what she felt was inappropriate material on some television programmes. Upset by the level of violence in the BBC programme *Eastenders*, she had written to the chairman of the BBC, and to every BBC governor, seeking an assurance that the BBC's rule not to transmit material unsuitable for children until after nine o'clock was still being followed.

"Since Mary Whitehouse said Eastenders was disgusting Richard's in there half an hour before it starts."

Sunday Express, November 17, 1985

Robin Day, a political broadcaster and commentator, was a forceful and popular presenter of the BBC programme *Question Time* which discussed political issues. The reference in the cartoon is to a high-profile and protracted court case, involving a prominent politician, at which high libel costs were being mentioned.

"Gentleman at the back – with libel costs at £500,000 a go, please be careful!"

Daily Express, October 23, 1986

The Singing Detective, by Dennis Potter, was a television serial with a very complicated and difficult story line. The serial met with considerable praise from the critics and proved to be very influential within the television industry.

"This year's play has nothing that a couple of scenes from The Singing Dectective couldn't improve."

Daily Express, December 9, 1986

Princess Diana was referring to the television programme in which four "royals" – Prince Edward, the Princess Royal, the Duke of York and the Duchess of York, each had a team raising money for a different charity. It was filmed at Alton Towers in Staffordshire and was broadcast three days later.

"They've come straight to Ascot from filming 'It's a Knockout'."

Daily Express, June 16, 1987

The Pub

One of many such pubs in Portsmouth at the time. It had just been announced that an American admiral was about to be appointed as commander-in-chief in the Atlantic, including ships of the Royal Navy, causing great consternation in Britain. A compromise was agreed two days later with a supreme American commander in the North Atlantic and, under him, a British admiral commanding the East Atlantic and an American admiral controlling the West.

"Bing Crosby as First Lord of the Admiralty – that'll be the day."

Sunday Express, February 25, 1951

A typical country pub of the type which would have been well-known to Giles. War-time rationing, particularly of food, continued many years after the end of the war and meat rationing did not finally end until July 1954.

"A few night-guard duties in Squire's woods'll help the meat ration – 'Halt. Who goes there?' No answer. Bang! And down comes a pheasant."

Sunday Express, November 18, 1951

This is the Fountain pub at Tuddenham – one of Giles's locals. The policeman was no doubt involved with a protracted railway strike which finally ended three days later. The clock appears to show that it was five minutes to midnight – well after closing time.

"If it ain't Bert Higgins! And us thinking he be up in Lunnun on strike duty."

Sunday Express, June 12, 1955

Aneurin Bevan, in a pub, somewhere in deepest Wales. Earlier that week, he had been elected Labour Party treasurer. *The Social Accounts of the Welsh Economy 1948–1952* had just been published in October, which prompted debate about Wales's financial role within the United Kingdom.

"Listen, Dai. When we've got them nicely tied up on Suez, Cyprus, wages, cost of living, you stand up and start hollering Home Rule for Wales."

Sunday Express, October 7, 1956

A pub interior showing a wide social range of clientele but with the game of cricket providing a unifying factor.

"I dare you."

"We'll draw our club money, have a few here, push on to the Spotted Cow, have a few with old Harry, move on to the Dog and Duck, have a couple with Sid, give the Queen's Arms a look, nip round to the Purple Lion ..."

Sunday Express, November 24, 1957

66   It had been announced that Princess Margaret and Antony Armstrong-Jones were to be married on 6 May that year – obviously the Welshman in the pub wished to make the most of it.

"Why I have to keep buying Taffy drinks just because everyone in his home town isn't called Morgan Evans is called Jones I'm ******** if I know."

Sunday Express, February 28, 1960

"If they made us stay open till 6 a.m. I know one of 'em who'd come creeping in five minutes before we close."

Sunday Express, November 13, 1960

68 At this time, in St Ives in Cornwall, there was considerable debate in some quarters about the increasing drift of 'beatniks' to their town. One local artist wrote in the local paper – "St Ives landlords have stated that they would never refuse to serve a drink to a genuine artist, and the trouble has been caused by bearded strangers whose occupation cannot, instantly, be 'pinned down'."

"I assure you, sir, that I am a VERY genuine artist."

Daily Express, April 11, 1961

A pub on market day, based on one in Ipswich which Giles, a farmer, would have frequented when attending the market there. Two days earlier, at the end of long agricultural negotiations, the European Commission had agreed to accelerate the introduction of the Customs Union and the Common Agricultural Policy.

"Can't you see 'em – Common Market all the morning, Folies-Bergere all the afternoon!"

Daily Express, January 16, 1962

General Charles de Gaulle, President of France, had just vetoed the British application to join the EEC.

"Agreed then – we send a note to de Gaulle telling him if he don't like Britain this club is cancelling its annual day-trip to Boulogne."

Sunday Express, February 10, 1963

Early 1963 was a highly significant period in the story of the Cold War years. In early February, Kim Philby defected to Moscow. Philby was part of a group which had all met as students at Cambridge University, including Donald Maclean, Guy Burgess and Anthony Blunt, who all became spies working for Russia. They were all cultured men who rose up through the ranks of the British diplomatic and intelligence services. It was revealed that considerable spy activity had been taking place at various trade shows and delegations. Blunt was extremely well known in museum circles, considered one of the most prominent British art historians of the time, and became the director of the Courtauld Institute in London and curator of the Royal Collections. Obviously Giles felt that information more useful to the Russians could be found in the typical British pub.

"In half an hour in a country pub the Russians would learn far more about the British than in all the museums and trading centres in the land." "I'll say they would."

Daily Express, February 26, 1963

"That last verse of yours not only mucked our chances of an Arts Council grant – it probably lost me my licence"

Daily Express, October 19, 1965

This cartoon shows the typical pub as a debating chamber. The fifth round of the FA Cup was played the day before. If, in fact, this cartoon was influenced by Ipswich (Giles's team) having drawn 1–1 away at Manchester City the day before, then the atmosphere in the pub would have been a lot more subdued two days later, when Ipswich lost 3–0 at home in the re-play.

"This'll liven up the post-mortem on yesterday's match – one of 'em wanting to know why the coach messed off home without him."

Sunday Express, March 12, 1967

This could be Giles drawing his worst nightmare – a pub full of families.

"Two iced lollies and a packet of bubbly gum ruddy well isn't what I ordered."

"And bang goes the Lounge trade."

Sunday Express, February 18, 1968

76   It was explained in an Old Bailey court that a CID officer had worked undercover wearing a dark suit, blue shirt and a white tie with polka dots, described as his "professional killer" outfit. The judge told the detective that "it was the best acting which would deserve an Oscar in any other theatre" and added, "I can only hope that the theatre will not be liable to entice you away from the forces of law and order."

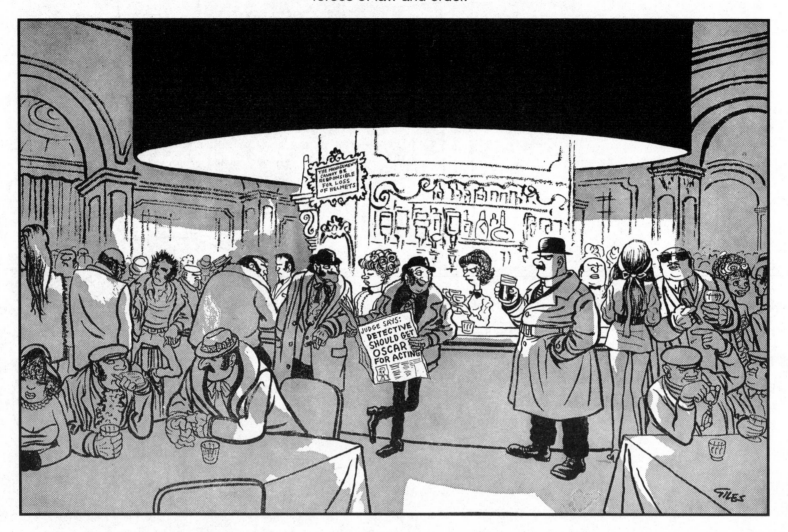

"'Evening, Hamlet."

Sunday Express, January 12, 1969

After nearly two weeks of strike the dockers no doubt were expecting some level of support from their pubs, but many publicans were experiencing their own problems with the large brewers.

"Closing our local while we're on strike is not the kind of support we're looking for, laddie"

Sunday Express, July 26, 1970

"Here we are, pundits, opportunity knocks. 'Liverpool and Leeds want the best manager money can buy to follow two of the most successful men in the history of the game'."

Daily Express, July 14, 1974

"This is me Solicitor, me Junior Counsel and me Senior Counsel – now let's see what sort of change we get this time,
yer thieving old trout."

Sunday Express, October 12, 1975

Giles picked up on the coincidence that the breaking news of the Guards' sex scandal story fell almost on the anniversary of Nelson's death.

"Sergeant, shall we stroll over and remind them that it was on this very day someone in the Navy coined the phrase 'Kiss me, Hardy'?"

Daily Express, October 21, 1975

"Aren't you the wee football fan I thumped for kicking up a row during our carol service?"

Scottish Daily Express, December 27, 1976

The typical British pub can be a dangerous place sometimes.

"Two large Sommes, two large Ypres, one large Passchendaele, one large Nijmegen, 3. 84 pounds."

Sunday Express, November 13, 1977

"Morning Charlie. I hear thou didst commit a sin that passeth all understanding by thrice placing the ball in your own goal during the first match of the season."

Sunday Express, August 20, 1978

This cartoon emphasizes some profound differences in the typical pub scene since Giles began his drawing career – a more family-friendly approach and the "gastro pub" concept, resulting in a retrograde change in the basic atmosphere in his opinion.

"Get him off my chair."

Daily Express, February 11, 1982

The Church

"Very well! Heads we have the village hut for 'Comforts for Korea', tails you have it for the anti-atom brigade."

Daily Express, August 1, 1950

"Vicar! On behalf of the Cornflower Water Colour Group I protest that allowing the Friends of Asia Painting Society to use the village hall the same day as us is carrying peace too far."

Sunday Express, April 12, 1953

"That's settled then, Vicar – all you have to do now is slip round and tell the Lady Dowager that little Miss Whatsit's going to open the fete instead of her."

A member of the House of Commons asked the Chancellor of the Exchequer, "in order to stagger the rush of weddings that take place in March so as to claim income tax relief for the whole of the financial year, will he give consideration to extending the period for three months during which the same relief can be obtained by those who prefer April, May, or June for the honeymoon period". He also added: "Is not the Minister aware of the difficulties expressed by clergymen who have to marry so many of these people with indecent haste, when it is their usual custom to have a talk with the couples before they get married?"

"A Reverend Shop Steward to see you, Your Grace."

Sunday Express, March 17, 1957

The Soviet Union entered the FIFA World Cup, hosted by Sweden, for the first time in 1958 and played England in their first game on this day – the result was a 2–2 draw.

"Ask vicar if we can have first and last verses only so you can get home for the England v U.S.S.R. match?
I most certainly will NOT!"

Sunday Express, June 8, 1958

"Sidney – did you put a bee in Miss Emily's Easter bonnet?"

Dr Michael Ramsey, Archbishop of Canterbury, had expressed the view that sermons should be livened up.

"While I appreciate Dr. Ramsey's comment that preaching is an entertainment, I consider giving your sermon on a trampoline was taking the matter too far"

Sunday Express, June 17, 1962

92 This probably relates to a decree, discussed at the Vatican Council taking place at that time in Rome, that there was an increasing need for high posts within the Church to be opened up to the laity. One bishop stated that "the Church should drop its 'clericalist' attitude and treat laymen as adults".

"Because somebody said Christians should not detach themselves from politics does not entitle you lot at the back to keep chanting, 'What about the old age pension'."

Sunday Express, October 11, 1964

Because of a series of breakdowns in services, parts of the country were experiencing severe restrictions on the use of gas and electricity.

"Best crowd we've had for months, thanks to gas and electricity cuts and my old coke heater."

Sunday Express, January 23, 1966

"Another big spending spree before the Budget – about three ha'pence a head"

Sunday Express, January 21, 1968

"You make the same mistake in the judging as they did with Miss England, boy, and I'll maim you."

Sunday Express, May 18, 1969

The previous day the newspapers reported that a shop owner in Carnaby Street, London was fined for a window display which included naked girls.

"Nude models may be right for Carnaby Street, Mrs. Barker, but not for the Ladies O.S. Stall, St. Botolph's Jumble Sale."

Sunday Express, June 1, 1969

"I told Vicar we intend to strike on Christmas Eve when it'll hurt most and he said the way we have been singing lately it was a good idea."

Sunday Express, December 20, 1970

The Union of Post Office Workers had voted for an all-out strike to start two days later in support of their pay claim. The Post Office denied reports that Post Office workers had been ordered to give pools coupons priority over other mail as the postal strike date approached.

"I wouldn't fancy our striking postmistress's chances of having her trepasses forgiven if Vicar's pools don't reach their destinations on time."

Sunday Express, January 17, 1971

"I would remind you that All Good Gifts Around Us have been carefully checked before the sermon."

Sunday Express, October 1, 1972

100 On 20 January 1974, English teams played league football on a Sunday for the first time. The Football Association, along with several clubs and players, had expressed support for Sunday matches earlier in the season, hoping that the move would help improve declining attendances, but they faced two obstacles: the Sunday Observances Act barred the selling of tickets on Sundays and there was some public opposition on religious grounds.

"Well that's all right lads. 11.0 Matins; early lunch; kick-off 3.0; back here by 5.30; wash and brush up and a cup of tea; Evensong 6.30."

Daily Express, January 8, 1974

The General Synod of the Church of England had just passed the motion: "This Synod considers that there are no fundamental objections to the ordination of women to the priesthood".

"I must say a Reverend 36-24-36 wouldn't be a bad idea, eh Harry?"

Sunday Express, July 6, 1975

"I don't have to remind you that the £ rose in stature at the closing of the Market on Friday, thereby enabling you to cough-up a higher percentage than you did last week."

Sunday Express, June 6, 1976

The summer saw a severe drought and a very strict ban on wasting water was imposed with a fine of up to £400 for anyone who was caught breaching the ban. The downpour the nation was praying for finally arrived on the August bank holiday and by October it was raining regularly.

"Oh Lord, forgive him, he knows not that he committeth an offence that doth carry a four hundred pound fine or one month, or both such penalties"

Daily Express, August 19, 1976

A national bread strike started four days before this cartoon appeared.

"In case anybody has any evil designs on our solitary loaf, curate will be riding shotgun, as it were"

Daily Express, September 11, 1977

"Daddy, I think Mrs. Montpelier-Smythe heard you say, thanks to her rock cakes, building may now commence."

Sunday Express, July 15, 1979

It had just been reported that St Paul's Cathedral would cover, in full, the costs of up to 34 boy choristers' tuition fees at the adjoining Cathedral School, in return for the boys' and their families' commitment to fulfil the particularly demanding musical programme at St Paul's. It was pointed out that the choristers needed to live at the school in order to fulfil their chorister role, so there were boarding fees to pay in addition to the tuition fees, now to be paid for by the Cathedral.

"I told him we wouldn't sing unless he paid us the same as St. Paul's Choir and all he said was 'Thanks'"

Sunday Express, July 19, 1981

Robert Runcie, Archbishop of Canterbury, had given a sermon of reconciliation and penitence at the Thanksgiving Service after the Falklands War, which gave rise to considerable criticism from some politicians and others. It had been expected that his address, given at St. Paul's Cathedral, would focus on triumphalism rather than reconciliation, whereas he declared: "People on both sides of this conflict are mourning", and asked the congregation to pray for the dead on both sides, and for Argentinian, as well as British, mothers who had lost sons.

"We're sticking to the old routine – look what happened to Runcie last week when he tried talking peace"

Daily Express, August 3, 1982

The Sinclair miniature television set, measuring 14 x 9 x 3 cm (5½ x 3½ x 1¼ inches), was launched two days earlier.

"Right! Before the service – all new miniature televisions up sleeves on table!"

Sunday Express, September 18, 1983

This refers to the removal of the £1 note and the future use of the £1 coin only – there was some public concern that this would lead to confusion, as illustrated here by Grandma.

"If you accidentally put a pound coin in the kitty by mistake that's your bad luck, mate!"

Sunday Express, November 18, 1984

Football

"Dear me, how time flies – football here already."

Daily Express, August 31, 1946

"Leaving tactics for a moment – I thought you might like to see a close-up of the gentleman who was calling you 'Big-Head,' 'Fairy-Feet' and so forth all through Saturday's match."

Sunday Express, August 21, 1955

It was generally considered that the recent budget helped the bosses rather than the workers.

"We'll have to lower their entrance price out of our tax relief – we're getting more 'Boos' than the ref ..."

Daily Express, April 11, 1957

During the 1950s, the maximum wage for professional football players was steadily increased and in 1957 it was raised from £15 to £17 per week.

"What do we do – get up there and bash 'em or pick it up?"

Daily Express, September 19, 1957

114 The Wolfenden Report drew attention to serious shortages in training and other facilities in many sports and leisure activities in Britain and listed a number of areas where improvements should be made.

"Well, I'm certainly glad you brought me along to see what the Wolfenden Committee wants the taxpayer to subscribe £5,000,000 towards."

Sunday Express, October 2, 1960

"Wasn't the one with the cap supposed to stop the ball going in the net?"

Sunday Express, January 8, 1961

On 18 January 1961, the wage restriction for footballers that had previously capped their earnings at £20 per week was finally removed. The wage limit was one of the concerns that nearly prompted a player strike in January 1961 backed by the Professional Footballers' Association and its chairman at the time, Jimmy Hill.

"Should be a good game."

Daily Express, January 17, 1961

The winter of 1962–3 (also known as the Big Freeze of 1963) was one of the coldest winters on record in the United Kingdom with temperatures plummeting and lakes and rivers beginning to freeze over.

"I bet Charlie's cold in goal today. By the way – where is Charlie?"

Daily Express, January 22, 1963

Three days earlier Alfredo di Stefano was kidnapped at gunpoint from his hotel in Caracas by members of the Venezuelan National Liberation Front. He was released two days later at the Spanish Embassy.

"Leave the doors open, Harry"

Daily Express, August 27, 1963

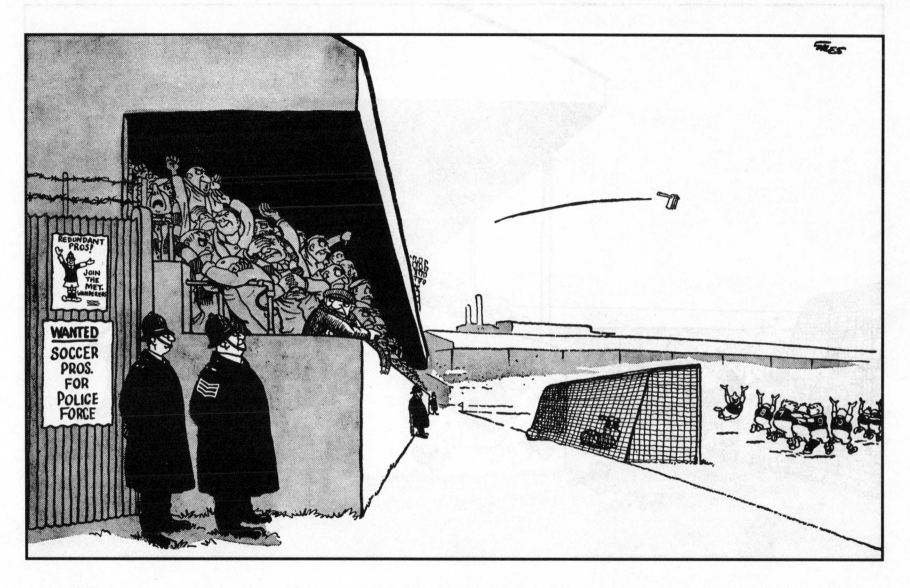

"He any good to you?"

Daily Express, March 5, 1964

Alistair's comments no doubt related to a decision taken a few years earlier to lift the £20-a-week ceiling on players' wages.

"Alistair! Why does it have to be you who bawls out you wouldn't pay £20 a week for the lot of them let alone each?"

Sunday Express, April 5, 1964

This was the period of a major betting scandal in English association football in which ten professional players were jailed for offences arising from match fixing.

"What makes you think it's our goalie throwing the match – why didn't they score?"

Daily Express, April 21, 1964

Following the Olympic Games in Tokyo, the Queen hosted the Great Britain and Northern Ireland team at a buffet luncheon at Buckingham Palace.

"Let another one through like that and I personally will see that you never attend a sportsmen's buffet lunch at the Palace."

Sunday Express, October 25, 1964

Unfortunately, the 1963–4 football season was marred by a series of foul tactics on the pitch, with the prefix "Dirty" becoming commonly attached to one major team.

"Cheek! I said 'Excuse me' before I belted him."

Sunday Express, November 22, 1964

On the 19 December, blizzards were reported in North Wales, North-west England and South-west Scotland. By 20 December, snow depths reached 30 cm (12 inches) on high ground in Scotland.

"Now there's a real fan – won't let a simple thing like the game being cancelled spoil his afternoon's sport."

Sunday Express, December 21, 1969

Football referees decided to be more determined in enforcing rigid control over matches and, the previous week, more than 30 players had their names taken, including six at Crewe and five at Tottenham.

"No, no, mummy – it wasn't the Ref who pushed me, it was this one over here."

Sunday Express, August 22, 1971

This cartoon probably relates to an incident involving Robin Friday, an English footballer who showed early promise but was known for excessive drinking and visiting nightclubs. In early December 1972, when he played for Hayes, his team started a match one player short because he had not turned up. When he finally arrived 80 minutes after kick-off, his intoxication was obvious but he was sent onto the pitch with the match still goalless and scored a late winning goal.

"I'll settle for a nice hot night club in exchange for training any time you like."

Daily Express, December 10, 1972

"Nice example you set – bopping their skipper just because he won the toss."

Sunday Express, August 17, 1975

"So I awarded you a free kick – but referees come under the new no-kissing law like everyone else. Git orf!"

The Union of European Football Associations (UEFA) had ordered that West Ham's return match, at home in the European Cup Winners' Cup against Spanish club Castille, should be played behind closed doors as punishment for "uncivil action" taken by their fans at the first-leg match at Castille. UEFA stipulated that a maximum of 140 people could be present at the game, including the players of both teams. West Ham won the game 5–1, making an aggregate score in their favour of 6–4.

"If we haven't got any spectators who threw that bleedin' bottle?"

Sunday Express, September 28, 1980

130   William "Billy" Bremner was a Scottish professional footballer noted for his captaincy of Leeds United during the 1960s and 1970s. In February 1982 he was awarded £100,000 libel damages after he successfully sued the *Sunday People* newspaper regarding an article that appeared in September 1977 claiming that he tried to fix football matches.

"They said that about my parents? That's good for a £100,000 libel!"

Sunday Express, February 7, 1982

On 16 April 1983, out of the blue, Robert Maxwell, the Oxford United owner and millionaire publisher, announced that he wanted to fuse Oxford United together with local rivals Reading as one team to be named "Thames Valley Royals". To the massive relief of fans of both clubs, the deal collapsed.

"On the other hand I can't find a ruling that says if you merge two teams you can't play twenty-two men."

Daily Express, April 19, 1983

132　England was having a difficult patch but, in fact, won the match 1–0, with captain Bryan Robson (see next cartoon) scoring in the 81st. minute. Sir Ian Kinloch MacGregor, KBE was an industrialist, who became most famous in the UK for his robust conduct during the 1984–5 miners' strike while managing the National Coal Board. At a secret meeting between the Board and the miners' leaders in a hotel on the outskirts of Edinburgh he picked up a plastic bag from the passenger seat, as his car drew up, and stepped out, placing the bag in front of his face. Peering out through the handles, he then walked silently into the hotel with the bag tight across his face.

"I should forget the plastic bags, Mr Robson – the way they're playing, I don't think the photographers will bother to turn up"

Daily Express, September 11, 1984

At this time Brian Clough was manager of Nottingham Forest and Bryan Robson played for Manchester United, where he became captain.

"Yes, I read Cloughie says footballers are worth £2,400 a week, but there's a wee GAP between Station Road Rangers and Bryan Robson."

Sunday Express, December 7, 1986

The standing ovation occurred two days earlier, following Margaret Thatcher's speech to the Conservative Party Conference in Brighton.

"Give him a standing ovation – 5-0 down and he puts another one in our own goal."

Sunday Express, October 16, 1988

Bobbies on the Beat

It is estimated that around 45,000 British girls married American servicemen during the Second World War. With the ending of the war the US authorities, understandably, were keen to get their servicemen home quickly and decided that GI brides may have to wait up to a year before joining their husbands in the States. In early October 1945 around 1,000 of them marched to the US Embassy to protest at the delay. The demonstration was successful, the US authorities relented and the length of their wait was significantly reduced.

"Says he's as much right here as they have – married an American Red Cross nurse or something."

Daily Express, October 11, 1945

Following an extended period of extremely hot weather in May and June, with temperatures of over 30°C (86°F), there was a second heatwave in July.

"Don't take you long to turn a heat wave into a crime wave, do it?"

Daily Express, July 15, 1947

This is a reference to an extremely successful film at the time entitled *The Third Man*, with Harry Lime as the principal character. The film centred on spies operating in Vienna with some scenes involving the older parts of the city's sewerage system.

"Come on out, Harry Lime."

Daily Express, December 7, 1949

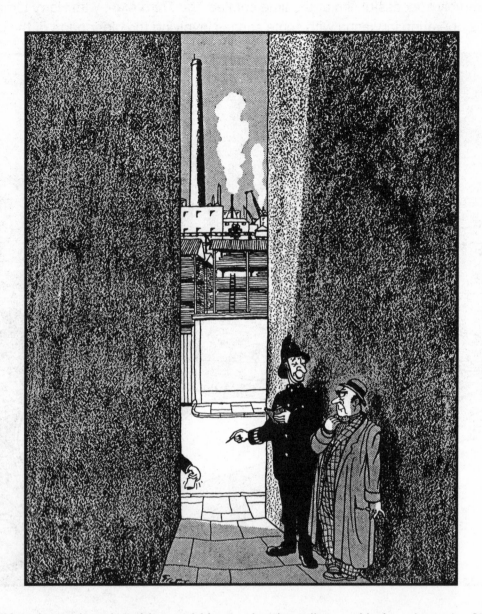

"Now I wonder what this would be – a betting-slip or a Hydro-plant plan?"

Daily Express, March 9, 1950

"Why fingers! We hardly recognised you."

Sunday Express, December 19, 1954

"Off home, all of you, before I charge you with being dressed in a manner likely to cause a breach of the peace."

Daily Express, January 1, 1957

"What time does your ship leave, Captain?"

Daily Express, January 1, 1960

Three days earlier the House of Lords considered a report from the Royal Commission on the police which recommended that the constable's pay should be initially £600 with a maximum of £990 in London.

"Since they've heard about our pay increase this is the third time I've been slugged and had me wallet whipped."

Sunday Express, November 27, 1960

"Just leave it there one minute over time my lad – that's all."

Daily Express, February 7, 1961

A grave national shortage of potatoes was discussed in Parliament earlier in the week and as a consequence foreign potatoes were shipped into the UK to help.

"Five ton of best potatoes. My! You've been busy on the old kitchen garden, Fingers."

Daily Express, April 17, 1962

"Now let's get this straight – you say he flicked a spoonful of hot chop suey at you so you flicked a spoonful of hot curry at him?"

Daily Express, November 22, 1962

Harold Macmillan had moved from 10 Downing Street to Admiralty House on 3 August 1960, initially for two years, to allow reconstruction work involving numbers 10, 11 and 12 Downing Street. Obviously the work had over-run.

"You've chained yourself to the wrong railings, Sir – the Prime Minister hasn't lived here since August 1960."

Daily Express, April 11, 1963

The day before the National Union of Bank Employees announced that they were calling for a one-day strike over a pay dispute at four different locations around the country. The Trustees Savings Banks chosen were branches in Manchester and Salford, Thames Valley, Falkirk and Monmouthshire. This was taking place at a time when Scotland Yard was making a massive attempt to locate the robbers involved in the Great Train Robbery 21 days earlier, when £2.5 million in cash was estimated to have been stolen.

"Now if Robin Hood will give us the names of the rest of his merry men who were going to knock off the bank to give to the poor bank clerks on strike..."

Daily Express, August 29, 1963

It had been reported that Parliament had discussed the recent unruly conduct of members during debates.

"Salute 'em! I'd put 'em across my knee and smack all their botwots."

Daily Express, February 4, 1965

"He's got a point – there isn't one that says 'No Fatstock'."

Daily Express, December 7, 1965

150   It was reported in London by the president of the National Hairdressers' Federation that barbershops and beauty salons soon would be replaced by unisex salons serving both men and women. He said "more and more British men have been going to beauty parlours to have their long hair styled".

"Looks like you've lost a couple of your short-back-and-sides, Horrie."

Daily Express, April 15, 1971

"This anonymous note saying you have a bomb on board – we have reason to believe it was sent by your wife who isn't very keen on sailing."

Sunday Express, May 30, 1971

This was a time of police understaffing in some parts of the country. The chief constable of one affected county in the South-east said that he was short of 396 officers and added that "more favourable income and acceptable hours of work were offered by outside employment".

"Watcha, Bertie – considering there is only one policeman for every 500 people in Britain you're a very lucky man.
I am about to give you my undivided attention."

Daily Express, June 17, 1971

Two years earlier Bernadette Devlin, then a 21-year-old Irish socialist and republican political activist, had become Britain's youngest ever female MP. She represented Mid-Ulster in Northern Ireland and was known as an extraordinary and uncompromising woman. The day before this cartoon appeared, she announced that she would fight another election, despite being pregnant, probably an unusual situation at that time.

"When I signed on for this job it didn't say anything about baby-sitting."

Sunday Express, July 4, 1971

154 The Osmonds were an American pop group consisting of four brothers whose popularity amongst young girls caused near riots when they appeared on stage. When they arrived at Heathrow airport two days earlier, as part of a European tour, several young female fans were taken to hospital with slight injuries after a wall collapsed following a crowd surge. The day before this cartoon appeared, the group performed at the Belle Vue in Manchester.

"Music hath charms, Charlie boy"

Daily Express, October 23, 1973

"Well, how was Princess Anne?"

Daily Express, August 19, 1975

The Silver Jubilee marked the 25th anniversary of Queen Elizabeth II's accession to the thrones of the United Kingdom and a number of Commonwealth countries. Celebrations culminated in June with a number of official "Jubilee Day" parties held around the country.

"Ladies! What would her Majesty say – just because you say your neighbour's hung on to three of your chairs and she says you've nicked six of her forks."

Daily Express, June 8, 1977

"You say the lady kissed your head under the mistletoe thereby causing you sexual harassment?"

Daily Express, December 21, 1982

158 Obviously a busy time for this group of policemen – dealing with demonstrations at the Greenham Common Women's Peace Camp and coping with the National Graphical Association picket line disputes and, here, trying to control the frenzied buying of the latest craze to arrive on our shores from the United States.

"Greenham and NGA pickets are enough for one week without bloody Cabbage Patch dolls."

Daily Express, December 1, 1983

"The new anti kerb-crawling Bill does not apply to us, Sir!"

Sunday Express, May 19, 1985

9

Carl Giles had been cartoonist for Lord Beaverbrook's *Daily* and *Sunday Express* for almost 20 years, when on 20 March 1962 the Conservative MP Sir Martin Lindsay tabled a motion deploring "the conduct of Lord Beaverbrook in authorizing over the last few years in the newspapers controlled by him more than 70 adverse comments on members of the royal family who have no means of replying".

Lindsay was wrong about the royal family having no means of reply. That day Prince Philip also vented his anger at Beaverbrook's campaign, during a press reception at the British Embassy in Rio de Janeiro. According to the paper's Brazil representative, the Prince declared that "The *Daily Express* is a bloody awful newspaper. It is full of lies, scandal and imagination. It is a vicious paper."

Prince Philip as a saint in a stained-glass window, drawn by Giles in 1961.

When the *Daily Express* reported this the next day, Giles decided to treat it as a joke. He knew the royal family enjoyed his cartoons; they often asked for the artwork. This had begun in 1948, when Prince Philip was sent a cartoon on the State Opening of Parliament, and over the next few years Giles received a steady stream of requests from Buckingham Palace for original drawings.

Giles drew the diminutive Lord Beaverbrook being escorted through the Traitor's Gate at the Tower of London, with a headsman's axe and block standing ready in the background (see page 17). The caption repeated Prince Philip's condemnation of the *Daily Express*, but added laconically: "'Ah well,' said Lord B., as they trotted him off to the Tower, 'at least he takes it or he wouldn't know it was a bloody awful newspaper.'"

This was a brilliant response, which did much to defuse the situation. When Giles's cartoon was printed the next day, *Daily Express* staff were surprised to receive a phone call from the Queen's press secretary, with a message for Giles that "Her Majesty requests today's cartoon to commemorate one of her husband's most glorious indiscretions."

Giles sent off the artwork and in May 1962 found himself invited to "a small informal luncheon party" at Buckingham Palace with the Queen and Prince Philip. "I was filled with absolute dread," Giles recalled afterwards. "But as soon as she started to talk I was put at my ease…There were about half a dozen corgis running about in a completely uncontrolled state. Suddenly the Queen shouted, 'HEP'. It was like a bark from a sergeant major. The corgis immediately stood to attention. Then filed out of the room."

After the lunch Giles mischievously drew a cartoon of the guests leaving with corgi-savaged trousers. He sent it to the Queen, who returned her thanks through one of her private secretaries, noting that she was "glad that you got away without having lost, at least to the best of her knowledge, so much as a shred of your trousers".

After that Giles became what one *Daily Express* journalist called "a kind of cartooning jester to the royal family". By the time he retired in 1991 the royal family had more than 40 of his original drawings, the largest number being owned by Prince Philip, who shared Giles' anarchic view of the world.